Rebuilding Life after Trauma

Tonya L. Whiteside

Copyright © 2013 by Tonya L. Whiteside

Rebuilding Life after Trauma
by Tonya L. Whiteside

Printed in the United States of America

ISBN 9781625099136

All rights reserved solely by the author. The author guarantees all contents are original and do not infringe upon the legal rights of any other person or work. No part of this book may be reproduced in any form without the permission of the author. The views expressed in this book are not necessarily those of the publisher.

Unless otherwise indicated, Bible quotations are taken from American Standard Version of the Bible.

www.xulonpress.com

Art work image of Tonya and an Angel
By: Rob Thornton
http://www.BRobArt.com

Photograph of Tonya L. Whiteside
By: Carla Rhea
Photographer/Artist
http:/www.carlarheakids.com
http://www.thefotoagency.com
http://www.carlarheaweddings.com
http://blog.iwanabnpix.com/
cell 714.273.6292
fax 714.508.6852

Dedication

*In loving memory of Stacey T. Bryant
(1972 – 2010)*

*"Give a girl the right shoes and
she can conquer the world."
Marilyn Monroe*

Stacey Bryant, Shoe Aficionado

Contents

Acknowledgements ix
Foreword. xi
1. Survey the Exterior Damage 19
2. Peel Back the Layers. 27
3. Examine the Cost 43
4. Keep Good Record of Repairs 51
5. Focus on One Rebuild at a Time. 69
6. Expect Aftershocks 77

Acknowledgments

Thank you Lord for my new life. I know my life has just begun. My rebuilding process could not be possible without the love and support of my husband, Earnest, and sons, Adrien and Andre. You are part of the reason why I keep trying. Thank you, family for letting me rebuild in my own way without judging my methods. You are so amazing, and I am so blessed to be a wife and mother. Thank you, Mom and Dad, for giving me life, love, and laughter. To my friend and victim's advocate, Laura, your friendship and spiritual support is beyond measure. Thank you for always sharing kind words, whispering prayers, and giving awesome hugs. I also want to thank my close friends both near and far for continuing to be there for me. Some of you have even seen my ugly cry. To my lifelong Hoptown Girls, thank you for listening early in the mornings and late at night, praying with me, and praying for me. I love you so much. Since our kindergarten years together, our bond has gotten stronger. Lastly, to my church family and the women of the finest sorority, Delta Sigma Theta Sorority, Inc., I cannot thank you enough for all the cards, phone calls, prayers, and visits. Your continued love and support is overwhelming and much needed as I move through every phase of rebuilding.

Foreword

"Rebuilding Life after Trauma" is a must read for all, especially for anyone who has experienced trauma or comforted someone who has been traumatized.

With the recent national media exposure regarding the massive killings in Newton, Connecticut at the Sandy Hook Elementary School, this book is timely and offers comfort and hope to the families that are left without their loved ones and trying to make peace with their loss.

Tonya takes us on a journey that begins with a series of unfortunate events that left her speechless and in shock while standing just inches away from her dear friend Stacey, who was shot in the head and killed in front of her eyes! Just moments later, more shots rang out and a second friend was lying dead also!

If you've ever wondered what you would do if confronted with such a tragedy, I guarantee you that you will be absorbed in the details to follow as Tonya speaks with candor and conviction as she vividly recalls the painful details of what took place in the garage on that hot summer day in such a breathtakingly beautiful community.

Tonya clearly understands that she was chosen for such a time as this. She takes the devastating loss of her two friends and makes a conscious effort to rebuild her life and to assist others by providing simple recovery steps to uplift and empower those that are having a difficult time coping with traumatic experiences.

I've never met anyone quite like Tonya Whiteside. She's a dedicated wife, loving mother, committed educator, counselor, and friendly neighbor. Her positive energy and enthusiasm is contagious. She dreams BIG dreams and encourages others to pursue their passion and purpose. I'm honored to call her friend and blessed to be in her presence. She is a constant reminder that all things are possible with God.

Respectfully,

Tanya Hutchison
Founder, Phenomenal Women, Inc.

INTRODUCTION

Boy has my life changed. I never thought I would be rebuilding my life in so many areas. Since being a victim and a witness to a murder suicide, I have been trying to find out how to live again. People say to me, "I don't know how you do it," or "I don't know what I would have done if I had been through what you have been through." The question that I am still learning to respond to is, "How are you?" Though the question is only three words, it is so hard to come up with an answer from moment to moment. What I can say is my answer is different just about every time I answer. One thing I do know is if I am going to truly respond to the question of how I am doing, I am going to have to tear down my walls and be exposed. If I am going to understand how I am doing, I am going to have to be open to the truth about me which will mean revealing insecurities, pride, fear, and the list goes on. I can say that I am doing better today than I was doing yesterday!

I had so many thoughts, so many emotions, hitting me all at the same time. Post-Traumatic Stress Disorder! Not me! I'm fine! I am a woman, and we cry for no reason all the time. Counseling? I'm fine, my husband is fine, and my children are fine. As I stood in shock over what had just happened, I just couldn't move. When others talk about what they would do in such a situation, the responses vary from "I would run," to "I would cover my face." Well I did neither. The shock and disbelief of it all had me paralyzed in the moment. Staring at a gun and it staring back at me was so overwhelming that I was only able to say, "Oh my God! Oh my God!" Even after saying this, I could not move. One thing I realize is I was not alone in that three-car garage. There had to be something or someone looking over me. How was I able to stand still? My life did not have a chance to flash before my eyes—as the old saying goes—yet I was afraid that I would not see my family again.

I want to examine my life with you, and if you find yourself in my story, I hope you will be able to answer the question of how you are doing. Once you can truly answer the question as I am doing, you will be able to live again. I have decided to tell myself the truth about me, because for me, this is the beginning of living again. If you find yourself in the process of rebuilding due to tragedy, loss of a loved one, heartache, divorce, addictions, or even physical illness such as cancer, we can do this together.

So how do you define trauma? One definition I found suggests that trauma is a serious injury or shock to the body, as from violence or an accident; an emotional wound or shock that creates substantial, lasting damage to the psychological development of a person, often leading to neurosis. Lastly, trauma is defined as an event or situation that causes great distress and disruption. Trauma does not have to define who you are and what kind of day you are going to have. Rebuilding life is a process, and though it may seem too much to endure at times, it can be done. I am determined to make my days great again.

It is my belief that we have the power and are responsible for feeding our brain. We choose from our thoughts what we are going to say and how we are going to say it. Invite those things and characteristics that worked for us in a positive and motivating way to be a part of our new day. Sure, there will be bumps along the way, but we can make the decision that it is going to be a great day. I truly recognize now that my life has been a life of preparation. This life, our life, is nothing but training for what is to come. We have a choice to act out our lives in any way we choose. So, we don't have to have regrets about not having the success we wanted. Take your experiences and make them work for you. I have had so many jobs, and there has not been one that I did not gain some experience from. In this book, I have chosen to share some of them with you because they are a part of my rebuilding. The military started me on the path of self-discovery, and this is where I must begin by revisiting basic training. And through the tragic and traumatic event of losing Stacey to domestic violence at the hands of her husband Eddie, I was reminded that I was trained to stand firm and stand brave. A string of part time jobs in the retail and customer service industry refined my personal values and ability to offer "service with a smile" even when it is difficult to smile. Nothing in my life is an accident. In everything, I give thanks.

Thinking Positive
Leads to
Speaking Positive.
Speaking Positive
Leads to
Believing Positive.
Believing Positive
Leads to
Living Positive.

Chapter 1

Survey the Exterior Damage

The headline of the Orange County Register read, "Friend was in house where 2 were killed... The unidentified friend and the next door neighbor both called 911... It looks like relationship problems," one officer said. "Despite the apparent relationship problems, there was no hint of trouble before the deadly shooting..."

So, did I miss something in the very beginning of my relationship with Stacey and Eddie? I was a young military wife when I met Stacey. My husband was active in the Marine Corps and I was in the Army Reserve. We had not lived in California that long when we were introduced to each other. I was first introduced to Stacey by a mutual friend, and our relationship grew. That evening, we gathered in the small living quarters in military base housing. My husband and I were beginning to make friends with couples in the military since we didn't know very many people after relocating to California. I never thought I would live in California nor be the wife of a Marine, but I settled into my new role with the support and friendships that included Stacey and Eddie. Being a military wife took some time for me to get used to. Stacey seemed to be preoccupied in a phone conversation most of the night, stating, "This is my husband Eddie, and he is out of town."

I remember telling my husband, "Stacey is so bubbly, even when she is talking to her husband on the phone. It is nice seeing young love!" Months passed before we saw each other again. We met again at our mutual friend's home on the military base, and once more, Stacey mentioned Eddie being out of town. I thought to myself, "Eddie is such a busy man. I hope we get to meet him soon." It would be months later that I meet Eddie. Boy was he muscular and very fit. I cannot remember the exact event, but he seemed nice. Eddie was very quiet and a bit reserved in comparison to Stacey. We had a good time laughing and getting to know one another. It turns out Eddie was a former Marine, so he and my husband, along with the other military men, had lots to talk about. They shared stories and even from time to time realized they had spent time in some of the same places and knew some of the same people. A year or two had passed, and now Stacey and I were even closer. She supported all of my entrepreneurial adventures. From selling Tupperware to Mary Kay, oh I cannot forget the

Tahitian Noni Juice and Partylite candles; Stacey was always one of first to order and book a party.

From planned weekend getaways and business trips, Stacey was always on the go. She would talk about how much she wanted to travel. I just loved her energy, but more importantly, she loved to have her family come to visit her in California. She and Eddie would always take them to see the sights and end the visits by having small gatherings. In their home, we would have what I call good ole family bonding. Stacey's family as well as Eddie's family welcomed me and my family. I miss them all very much as I feel like I have lost them as well. Maybe one day we will find our way back to one another. When Stacey and Eddie purchased their first home, it was only ten miles away from our apartment. We spent more time together whenever she was not traveling. Eddie took a job in northern California for a short time, and I was so hoping she would not move away. When they decided to sell their first home because it was too small, my son and I would keep her company while Eddie was away. We would talk about her finishing school and wanting to move up in positions at her job. Stacey loved her company and even told her boss that one day she wanted to be the boss. Stacey did achieve that goal because of her hard work and commitment to service. I never heard her say one bad thing about her company. She worked with passion and personally cared about all of the people she supervised. I honestly do not know, looking back, how Eddie felt about all of Stacey's success. I really hope he was as proud of her as we were. Things just continued to fall into place for Stacey.

The company where Stacey was employed gave her the flexibility to hire contractors for various projects. I was one of them. As a Career Consultant and Workshop Presenter, Stacey would bring me in for new hire orientation to train management, leadership, and hiring practices. I would also travel out of state to business conferences, offering team building, self-assessment, and goal setting workshops. Eddie would always be there in the background. So were the signs there that, in years to come, something unimaginable would happen? Couples have disagreements and an occasional argument, and I do not think that is strange at all. A realization I have come to in the last few years is that domestic violence may be something you never see on the outside. In this case, I never saw it. Other people have gone on to say that yes, there was in fact abuse in Eddie and Stacey's marriage relationship. What I am here to tell you is that on the outside, in the earlier years, Stacey never once said anything negative to me about her husband Eddie. She was an excellent wife and dynamic business woman.

Survey the Exterior Damage

So when did the bottom fall? July 28th, between breakfast and lunch. That was when I hit bottom. My mind that morning was mentally preparing for the road trip to the conference in Las Vegas with Stacey, founder of this non-profit organization. Though I would miss my husband and the boys those few days, I was looking forward to some much needed time away. Stacey and I had spoken about what my role was going to be at the annual conference. My responsibilities normally included organizing and creating the opening activities and energizers throughout the weekend. Stacey had some great ideas for activities and was so cheerful and excited as she shared with me her thoughts. I explained that I was looking forward to having a room to myself which would provide me with much needed quiet time and relaxation between sessions. She said that was going to be fine because, after all, it was a spa resort.

I was waiting to hear from Stacey because the plan was that I was going to meet her at her home to pack the car and ride to Vegas. Since she had just flown in from out of town, I thought maybe she was taking care of errands. While waiting, I asked my family to gather so we could pray together before I went out of town. Since we were not pressed for time, I took the opportunity to speak over each one of them. I remember thanking God for my family and for their uniqueness. Now that I am going through a rebuilding phase, I am learning to enjoy the small things, the many blessings, the similarities and differences within my children even more. My husband and I are even dating again, but that is in the next book...

My crazy and hectic life prior to beginning the rebuild was filled with many days of over-commitment. My day began at 5:30 a.m. during the week. Well, my alarm clock would go off for the first time at 5:15 a.m. Depending on how well rested I felt, I might have only hit the snooze once, but there were those mornings where I would hit it three or four times. Now, I didn't go back to a deep sleep, but I would doze off a bit. I began to plan my day before I was even out of bed. I thought about what day of the week it was, did I have any early morning meetings, were there any after school activities for the boys. I thought about people I needed to email, text, call, meet with and, most importantly, what was I going to wear. My drive to work after dropping off the kids was pretty uneventful, and often I was able to pray and meditate. I was happy to clear my mind and mentally prepare for work. Stacey and Eddie had been our friends for over 15 years. After seeing my friend murdered by her husband, I now have to find a way to not replay that scene in my head over and over as I drive to work. It will take some time to move through the damage that took place. My quiet time just is not the same as it used to be. My thoughts have been invaded, and I am learning how to deal with the distractions that come with the silence. My heart has been broken, and some of my relationships have been lost. But I can no longer mask my emotions in my outward appearance since trauma can have you to re-live certain moments in time over and over and over. Life threatening situations will impair our senses at times and cause us to lose focus. But staying focused on my personal rebuild is a drive worth taking.

Rebuilding life requires a review of the structure and foundation

Chapter 2

Peel Back the Layers

Pacing back and forth on the sidewalk and frantically waiting for help to arrive is all I could do while on the phone with 911. I hear the operator ask me to stay calm and move away from the home until I feel like I am in a safe place. "Help is on the way," the operator says. I say to the operator the same words I uttered to the neighbor, to my husband, and to one of our close friends, "Eddie just shot Stacey! He shot her! Then he shot himself! Please come quickly!" The neighborhood police do arrive very quickly, and one of them walks me over to the sidewalk clear of the home about two houses down. The officer asked, "Do you know who is in the home and if they are armed." Of course, I said frantically that, "Yes! Eddie just shot Stacey, and I believe he shot himself in the living room of the home. Please go check on Stacey! She is in the garage!" I watched as at least half a dozen officers suited up and prepared to enter the home. I thought I was going to pass out, but having a friend arrive just as the caution tape was going up really helped me catch my breath. She placed her arms around me and held me close. Breaking through my tears, I uttered, "I just cannot believe this is happening."

As I sat on the curb on Birdhollow, I couldn't think straight. My mind was racing, my hands were shaking, and my heart was pounding so hard in my chest. An officer approached to ask how I was doing and told me that as soon as the detectives interviewed me, I could leave. Helpless, I had to sit and wait to be interviewed. Meanwhile, my friends were still inside the home, and I did not know how they were doing. I heard sirens which meant help was on the way. I saw the police officers knocking down a beautiful red front door, and I knew that just beyond the door was a fine-looking baby grand piano. Stacey once told me she used to take piano lessons and Eddie bought her the piano. She planned to start lessons again. Now I could hear the paramedics say that one of the victims was still breathing. "Oh my God! Is it Stacey?" I asked my friend who was consoling me, "Could Stacey still be alive?" Now I was having thoughts that just maybe if I had stayed with her in the garage, she would have had a better chance of survival. I started to think about where she was lying in the garage and if the paramedics were able to find her. "Please, Lord, let her live!" I cry out, "Please, Lord, let Stacey live!" In the time that seemed like hours, I had to sit on the side and just wait.

The officers asked me not to make any more phone calls which meant I could not talk to my husband or my children. My husband was far away on a job assignment, and by the time he made it back through traffic, the street was closed to him. Friends were able to get a message to me that he was there, and every one of them was praying. I felt like I was back in basic training and, even more, I felt like I was at war. I joined the Army Reserve right out of high school and was put on alert during the Desert Shield and Desert Storm wars. I spent eight years of my young adult life preparing for battle. Witnessing the death of two friends was just like being in a war. What I have discovered is that rebuilding life requires a review of the structure and foundation. I was trained to be a soldier in time of war, and by all accounts, this was war. Though it had been a while, I think your mind, your body, and your instincts can remember what to do. If I want to rebuild I have to go back and revisit where it started for me by examining my foundation.

1988 was a finally here! My high school graduation was just around the corner, and my army basic training was a few weeks away. My friends were preparing to leave for summer school away at college, but I would have to wait until summer was over because duty was calling. I had dreamed of this moment. I was finally moving away from home and venturing out on my own. Military police, here I come!!!! I was ready! I was in the best shape of my life. Having been an athlete since the seventh grade had prepared me for the Army Reserve Boot Camp. My goal was to be successful at Fort McClellan, Alabama and use the Montgomery GI Bill money to pay for college. I knew I was going to have a career in the Criminal Justice field, and being a military officer was just the beginning I needed.

The home phone was ringing, and no one was jumping up to get it. I had to answer it; the Army Recruiter said he would call me to let me know when I would be leaving. "Hello," I said, "this is she. Hi, Sergeant, yes, I am listening. I have to be ready to leave this Saturday? Oh, yes, I am ready. It is not a problem to leave three weeks early. I will just explain it to my parents." Now at this point, my parents had been pretty calm. They were not overly happy that their oldest child and only daughter signed up for the army reserves. I think they understood why I did it. I didn't want to burden them with paying for college. I thought that I could prove to them I was now an adult making good choices. If I was going to be successful in life, this was the only way for me to move out, learn discipline, responsibility, and independence. Not to mention seeing things and going places I had only dreamed about. "Mom, Dad, you will never guess who was on the phone…"

As we drove away from our home, I couldn't help but think about my life as a child and teenager. I had most of the same friends since kindergarten. We loved each other so much, and there I was leaving. Was I doing the right thing? What if this was a mistake? Was it too late to change my mind? Oh no, where were those tears coming from? If they saw me crying, what would they do? I was going to close my eyes until we got to the bus station. This was a happy day; my new life was about to begin. Too late, my dad had just seen me crying. "Don't cry, it is going to be fine," he said. "Everything is going to be great, you will see." Thank goodness my mom was driving. She could not see my face. I did not want her to be sad. "Here we are, the bus station," said my mom. The moment had finally arrived, and we hugged, kissed, off I went.

This was so exciting! I couldn't wait to get to training! The airport was just across the highway, and my flight was early in the morning. I had better get some sleep because who knew how much sleep I would get when I finally got there. Wait a minute, I just thought of something. Outside of summer camp as a child and being in a crop duster plane flying over fields, I had never flown anywhere!!! Now I was nervous! I did not get much sleep. I don't know if it was anxiety about flying, leaving for basic training, or both. As I approached my terminal, I began to feel tense. I was trying so hard to be strong and courageous. Flying is the best way to travel. Millions of people do it every day. Today is not going to be any different.

There was my seat, and it was a window seat. Now I didn't know if I was going to like looking at how high in the sky I was, but there was a shade I could pull down if I needed to. Oh, here comes this nice looking elderly lady. She had the middle seat. I would be strong for her just in case she needs me. "We have been cleared for take off," the captain announced. Here we go, I said to myself, but now I was trembling and I think having a panic attack. I started praying and crying at the same time. I couldn't control it. After a few moments of that, it was evident, I was terrified of flying! "Would you like to hold my hand, young lady?" I was so embarrassed, but through my tears, I said, "Yes, thank you so much." This flight had to be the longest ever. "Please remain in your seats as we are running into a storm up ahead," said the captain. I was trying so hard to let go of this lady's hand, but not now. Not after that announcement.

Why was I so scared? I think it is because of the unknown. I couldn't see what was in front of me, and I do not believe I had ever experienced anything like that. As an eighteen year old, life was good through my teen years. I lived in the same community until age seventeen. I played point guard on my high school basketball team, I made it to the state track meet in several events, my friends and I hung out just about every weekend going bowling and to football and basketball games. Those events did not frighten me. We did not win every sporting event nor was I the best athlete. This was different. I did not know what was ahead of me. I had an idea and maybe that is what scared me. "Lord, please let me live through this turbulence. I promise to be good." As the plane landed, I couldn't help but be overjoyed that this flying experience was over. I thanked the elderly woman for helping me through my flight. She was so nice to hold my hand most of the flight. This definitely would be an experience I would not soon forget. Dorothy Thompson, an inspirational writer, once said, "Only when we are no longer afraid do we begin to live." Now that this plane is on the ground, I am ready!

My military orders said to look for the Alabama limousine. I was excited because I had never been in a limo before. I couldn't wait to tell my family about this. What a way to show up at basic training! In a limo! Now that I had been waiting for some time, I was starting to think something was wrong. I hoped everything was okay. It was hot out there in the waiting area. These are some of the biggest mosquitoes I have ever seen. I am going to go call the number listed on the back to make sure they know I am here in Alabama waiting. When my call is answered, I explained with enthusiasm that I had been waiting for quite some time and was wondering when my limo would be arriving. The woman on the other end explained that there were two other flights, and they would be landing shortly so to please be patient and stay by the curb. I thanked her for explaining and went back to the curb to wait. Shortly, I was joined by other young men and women. They, too, are looking for the limo. Someone yelled out, "Here it comes!" I didn't see a thing. It took me a minute to pick my face up from the ground. I realized that I had been looking for the wrong type of limousine. I was looking for a long black car that would seat about 10 or 12 passengers. What pulled up in front of me was a 30 plus passenger bus that read, "Alabama Limousine" along its side. Quietly and in my embarrassment, I said to myself, "This has to be some kind of mistake." Realizing that it was no mistake, we were quickly ushered onto the bus and off to our new beginning.

"Wow what a huge place! I cannot believe how many people are here. Oh no! Why are those boys crying? Why is she throwing up? Oh, Lord, what have I done!" As our names were called and we were told to line up, I was becoming more and more excited. I knew I was going to love being a military police officer! Well, being a military police officer was not going to happen. Sadly, I was told that I was not tall enough and could not be selected for the academy after basic training. Well, law enforcement was put on hold. "Are you kidding me? My recruiter never told me there were restrictions!" The other choices presented to me were office clerical and transportation. So which do you think I chose? "Truck Driving School, here I come!" My major in college is going to be Criminal Justice, and I cannot wait to start in the fall.

"Listen up!" shouted the Drill Sergeant. "I don't know what you girls are used to, but this is my house!" All I remember next is someone coming behind me and wrapping their finger around a piece of my hair that was hanging from under my hat. I felt warm breath on the back of my neck and then heard, "As long as you are in my training, Private, I do not ever want to see this piece of hair hanging out from under your hat."

"Yes, Drill Sergeant!" I said with a slight tremor in my voice.

"What did you say, Private; I can't hear you!"

"Yes, Drill Sergeant!!" I screamed from the top of my lungs. Boy was I nervous. For a second time, I started thinking I made a mistake. Well, I did not have time to think about my decision for long because we were quickly shuffled off to our respective living quarters. This was the beginning of a new day and a new career.

As the training went on, I became convinced that I made the right decision. I was learning how to be independent and the importance of hard work. I enjoyed getting up at four o'clock in the morning and running ten to twelve miles, doing hundreds of push ups and sit ups. This was the best time of my life. The turn of events occurred on weapons qualification day. I have such a small body frame standing a mere five-foot one and weighing about ninety pounds. My hands just did not enjoy holding a weapon, let alone shooting one. In every weapons qualifying course, I would fail. I was given squeeze balls to help strengthen my hands, and try as I might, it was just really difficult for me.

Now, there were no problems in the classroom instruction or even the physical fitness. I was often the one who would run with the captain in the morning workouts, retrieving those soldiers and motivating them to complete the daily runs. I also was a helper during our backpack hiking excursions. I would always have someone holding on to my backpack as we would climb steep hills. "Come on, you can do it! It's the last hill, Private!" Now, I did not always know if it was the last hill, but it was so encouraging for the soldiers that it did not even matter.

Okay, it was show time. This was the day to prove that I was ready to move on from the basic training to my individual specialized training. I had just completed the physical fitness test and was ready for the weapons qualification. My hands felt great, but I was starting to sweat. I kept looking at the faces of the ladies as they came off the range. Oh no, she was crying. Oh no, my palms were now very clammy. Okay, it was my turn. I steadied my aim and really focused my breathing. I closed my left eye and began to focus on the targets in front of me. "Lord, please get me through this," I whispered as I pulled the trigger. And all the rest is a blur…

As I was leaving the range to meet with the instructor, I was starting to get this sinking feeling. I was starting to think that I did not qualify. Not qualifying would mean no graduation, and then what would I do? I approached the instructor, and he looked me in the eyes and uttered words I would never forget, "You didn't make it soldier and will have to restart." Somehow, I knew he was going to say that. I began thinking about what I was going to do.

I couldn't restart because I was supposed to start college in August. How could this be? Great, now I would have to walk back to my barracks and everyone was going to know that I didn't make it. Somehow, as I drew closer, I became more confident. Sure, this was totally not what I expected. I had a plan. I was going to prepare for my performance on the shooting range as much as I was allowed. It was easier than I thought to share the news with my all my new friends, including the one who months later became my first college roommate. Though I would miss them, I was prepared to restart and have more time to work on strengthening my hands. The first tough lesson I had to learn was that rebuilding can often be very difficult, but I also learned that rebuilding does not have to be impossible. Even something great can be worth the wait.

Rebuilding life means reminding yourself daily of who you can be tomorrow and not just who you are today.

As graduation day from Army Boot Camp came for the group I originally started with, I watched them walk by and I smiled. What was really encouraging was that they smiled right back. They knew I would be okay. Accepting the fact that even though the activities of basic training would be the same, I told myself that I was going to be okay. Because rebuilding life means reminding yourself daily of who you can be tomorrow and not just who you are today. I decided not to focus on the message that my life plan had been altered. Remind yourself daily that maybe you do not win; maybe you do not get that promotion or a raise in salary, but tomorrow is a new day, so decide to make it great. That is where I chose to place my focus.

My motivation would have been really different had I focused on what some would call a failure. Instead I viewed it as an opportunity—an opportunity to be better. I already knew what to expect in the physical fitness and classroom instruction. I could really focus on the one area that was a weakness. The weeks passed by quickly, and it was time again for weapons training. This time, I felt different. I was more confident than ever that I was going to succeed. I listened and followed my weapons instructor's guidance as closely as I could. I carried my squeeze ball everywhere, and I had other Sergeants pulling for me. Lots of Drill Instructors had learned my name and by now began to encourage me quietly when they were not yelling and screaming at me during fitness training.

Show time! I walked up to the weapons line and steadied my aim. The targets looked really bright. I closed my left eye and steadied my breathing. I watched each and every target, and I thought I could even see my shots on the paper this time! As the end of firing my M16 rifle was called and I walked off the live firing range, moving towards my instructor felt good this time. I think I was even smiling. I do not know if I was anxious, but the line to stand before the drill sergeant seemed much longer than the first time. "Congratulations, Private, you earned your sharp shooter's badge. You are moving on to the next phase of your training." The famed artist and illustrator, Florence Scovel Shinn, once said, "If one prepares for failure, he will get the situation he has prepared for." Well, I was preparing for success. I saw myself accomplishing my goal. I was beginning to learn that life does not have to be perfect to be great.

"I did it! I am so proud of myself! I know the hard work is not over and that this is just the beginning, but I cannot help but be happy to have made it this far," I tell my mom and dad on the phone. "We are proud of you daughter", my parents say. It means a lot to hear that they are proud. The Army values have become a part of me. I now have a sense of who I can be. I have learned loyalty, respect, integrity, how to be selfless in my service, and how to have courage. I also now knew how to wash clothes because I did not know before. It is also my belief that we are all created in such a unique way and have various gifts, talents, and abilities. You did not have to be in the military for those, and, to me, this is evidence of being

Army Strong. Tell yourself that you know your life and your circumstances are not always perfect. Make it up in your mind that you can be victorious and have victory over your circumstances. Is there anything or anyone in your past that you feel has had an impact on who you are today as a person?

If I am going to rebuild my life, I have to go back to my basic training. Rebuilding does not always require you to forget everything from your past. Rebuilding may require you to revisit your past. I carry with me the Army Strong values, and I use them one at a time as needed. I have learned to stop, to think, to observe, to plan, and to proceed with safety. I am no different than anyone else. I have learned skills that will last me a lifetime, and I am going to trust in my training. Have you or anyone you know ever said or made the comment that their job was a dead end or "that was such a waste of their time?" What about, "I wish I would have never met that person"? Rebuilding can be, for you and for me, getting rid of those items. This may even be ridding ourselves of people that do not mean us well. Rebuilding means we can put those things that are no longer working for us in storage. We may need them again someday, so I am not saying throw them away.

Rebuilding requires a Mindset Makeover

Chapter 3

Examine the Cost

I recently have had to come to grips with the fact that I am recovering from depression. Me! When I researched, I found that depression is a condition of mental disturbance, typically with lack of energy and difficulty in maintaining concentration or interest in life. That was me! And Post-Traumatic Stress Disorder! How can that be? I am a very upbeat person. I love encouraging others to make it a great day. The truth is, ever since the day I witnessed the lives of two friends taken away, I struggled with things some people may feel should be easy to handle. It took months for me to listen to what I was telling myself, "I am okay; I am just a little sad today." This went on until I took a look at myself in the mirror. I had lost weight and totally was not sleeping. Depression had me thinking that I was okay and the doctors only wanted to make money off me by having me medicated. Well, let's see, I no longer want to be in crowded places and just being in closed places that even resemble having no way out causes me to have anxiety. The one that periodically is a problem is hearing the sound of a balloon popped. It just reminds me of the gunshots in the garage and triggers the memory of events of Stacey's death all over again. Oh, yes, it was time to seek the assistance of a professional. I was beginning to think that, in time, I would just feel better and things would go back to the way they were.

Have you found yourself at that crossroad? Have you ever thought, "Do I really need help?" Let's think for a minute. Were any of us born knowing how to walk? Most of us laid on our backs or bellies initially and then learned to crawl. There are some who went straight to walking. Some mothers have said, "They did not want their knees to touch the ground." I say to that the knees had to have touched the ground at some point for the baby to know that they did not like that feeling. Learning to do something new or looking at ourselves in a truthful way may be very uncomfortable. But like with infants when they are learning to walk, often times someone may be holding their hand as they take the first steps. The hand holding may only be for a little while.

I realized early in the rebuilding process that I kept going back into the garage in my mind where my life ended. How can I rebuild my life outside the garage if I keep going back inside? I still can't bring myself to physically drive down that street, Birdhollow, even though it is less than 5 miles away. Wait, it dawned on me! I don't have to! I just don't know what will happen for me mentally if I turn down that street. Will I remember all the caution tape or all the people on the side of the road by the media cameras? Will I begin to smell the gun powder or see the stained driveway that was inside the garage? I am just not ready to revisit Birdhollow, and I am okay with that.

Having a new outlook can make all the difference in the world. Rebuilding requires a "Mindset Makeover," and I am working on what motivates me. I know! My family! Can I work and care for my husband and children? When the job does not work out, keep your integrity and stay the course. I have had my share of jobs. I even worked on my college campus in the registrar's office. I had a veteran's work study position with my military unit, and I worked part-time at McDonalds until I graduated. As if I were not busy enough, I took part-time jobs at a video store and Pizza Hut all while being a fulltime college student. I viewed each one of those positions as opportunities. Each opportunity taught me something new. If you are unhappy in a job, then keep what you like about it and make sure on your next job you don't bring with you the things you didn't like about the old job. In my rebuilding, I often rely on past experiences, skills, and lessons learned. If we fail to see opportunities in our past experiences, we have made a decision to accept and settle. There has to be a mental shift in our thinking and in the way we do things.

The position at the video store was really something I fell into because my hours had been cut at Pizza Hut and it was next door. I was really having a good time and learning a lot about movies. The customers were friendly, and the staff was great to work with. To this point, I have not mentioned any dating in college. Well, I began having problems with a crazy guy I dated for two weeks. He began stalking me at work. Once I broke it off, he would call the store every few minutes to talk to me. Now, I had not been on this job long, so I needed to make a good impression. I think the manager enjoyed having me around, but I could tell the phone calls started to become a distraction because my productivity was slowing down. The manager would often ask me if everything was okay and if we needed to call the police. Of course, I said no because I thought I had everything under control. I was eventually fired. Fired! The first time in my professional part-time career! The manager was really nice about it. She spoke to me privately as she was handing me my final paycheck. It was at the beginning of my shift, and since I had nowhere else

Examine the Cost

to go, I opted to stay and complete my shift. I thank the manager for the opportunity.

My mind has replayed this situation so many times over the years because now that I have experienced trauma, I realize that the situation was not healthy. It was somewhat dangerous. Dr. Jill Murray, professor and licensed therapist, shares that when a woman is in a destructive relationship, there are so many feelings (fear, shame, guilt, confusion, desperation, anger, humiliation, and longing), and often when she makes the decision to leave the relationship, she believes and assumes that those feelings will magically disappear. I don't know the ins and outs of the relationship of Stacey and Eddie, but I do wonder if she experienced any of those traits. I did not want to have to worry that my life could be in danger. I know that worry is not good and that it can disrupt the everyday flow of life. Worry commands your attention and takes your mind off the positive things in life.

Some will say as I did, "I just do not have the time right now to focus on me. I have so many other responsibilities that I am responsible for. My children, my job, my bills…" We have to examine the cost of doing nothing. Some may think there is no cost, but, oh, there is. The cost is the anxiety that keeps you up late at night. The cost will have you depressed. The cost will have you experimenting with drugs and/or alcohol. The cost is the fear that has you paralyzed and unable to leave your home. The cost of doing nothing about the interruptions in your life will have you blaming yourself for what you are going through. Bible Teacher and famous author, Priscilla Shirer, says the way you respond to the interruptions you are facing will have a bearing on the direction your life takes next. "When you look back over your life a year from now, two years from now, ten years from now, will you have regrets or bitterness about the decisions you have made concerning your life?" The cost of doing nothing may be more than some can handle on their own.

A few weeks prior to Stacey's death, she told me that her and her husband and my friend, Eddie, were separated. I initially was shocked but soon thought that I would just be a good friend by listening to her and supporting her the best way I could. She sounded so happy. I could hear the smile in her voice. It was like she was a different person. Stacey was always in a great mood, but this time was really different. She shared with me all the fun she was having visiting her family in Texas, in Ohio, and in Detroit. At the time of our conversation, she was at the home of one of her nieces. Her love for family was beyond measure. One of our close friends and I discussed our concerns about Stacey. We made a vow that we would be praying for both her and Eddie. In another of my conversations with Stacey, I asked her if she felt safe. I was very uncomfortable asking, but I do not think I would have been a good friend if I did not ask. Of course, Stacey did not tell me she felt afraid. She and Eddie were high school sweethearts and had been married 19 years. She said, "Oh, girl, of course not. You know Eddie. He would not hurt me." Though I knew Eddie could sometimes have a temper, he really did seem to love Stacey very much. Who am I to question their relationship? From the outside, I saw two people who loved and supported one another.

Rebuilding may result in bumps and bruises. Even small steps and little triumphs along your path will take on greater importance. Rebuilding life means telling yourself the truth about yourself

Chapter 4

Keep Good Records of Repairs

"I think I am going to need medication," is what I finally told myself. What are you telling yourself? Are you somehow convinced that your problem or situation is like no one else's? Are you good at balancing your life, or have you experienced a few setbacks like I have? Do you indulge in certain behaviors a little too much? If I were to have a conversation with the person you feel knows you best, what would he or she say about you if you were not present? If the two stories do not match up, it may be time to face facts. Success in one's life is not easily achieved without setting goals. If we never look at ourselves in the mirror, we may never be able to tell ourselves the truth. Often times, we do not want to ask the experts for help. If we want to accomplish anything worthwhile, we must be prepared and committed to take action.

Rebuilding may result in bumps and bruises. Even small steps and little triumphs along your path will take on greater importance. Rebuilding life means telling yourself the truth about yourself. Depression does not always let me enjoy the small things and tiny blessings, but I am fighting to regain all of those freedoms. I looked death right in the face. I saw one loved one take the life of another loved one, yet in the midst of being faced with death, I did not feel I was alone. The memories are hard; my healing is hard, but in the core of it all, I never lost my praise. Sometimes I cry, sometimes I say nothing, but I know I will be victorious. Former first lady Eleanor Roosevelt once said, "You can gain strength, courage, and confidence by every experience in which you really stop and look fear in the face. You must do the thing which you think you cannot do." I have accepted the challenge to do just that. There is not just one way to rebuild life after a traumatic experience. I have found out over the years in more than one instance that my marriage and raising my children is not the same as anyone else's. What is traumatic for me may not be for you, and I had to accept that fact, though it has been difficult. At times, I do wish my family and friends knew just how I hurt. I know that my friends and family have their own trauma and experiences and that we all process things in different ways, but we are all different. The realization in all of this is my pain is personal. One thing that we all have in common is we all want to have victory over our circumstances. What I mean by that is we all, at one time or another, have to let go of emotional baggage. We just do not think we have the power to do so, or we just do not want to put in the effort. Thomas Edison once said that, "If we did all the things we are capable of, we would literally astound ourselves."

Rebuilding life requires meditation day and night

My daily devotional time is so important to my healing and rebuilding. I have to retrain my brain to focus on what matters the most. My eyes, ears, nose, and mouth need a new start to meditation. What my eyes witnessed was something horrific. What my ears heard was shocking. I can still smell gun smoke from time to time, but I never get tired of using my mouth to thank God. It was a process because I found it hard to accept that my life was spared. When you see on the television and hear in the media of domestic violence in the home, most often no one survives. I am not thanking God just because He spared my life because I truly believe I died that day in the garage. There was no way I could be the same me. I thank God that I have a new opportunity to live out a new purpose for my life. A bible verse that has become part of my healing is **Matthew 9:17, "Neither do men put new wine into old wine-skins: else the skins burst, and the wine is spilled, and the skins perish: but they put new** *wine into fresh wine-skins, and both are preserved."* Though this scripture was written explaining that Jesus came not to patch up an old religious system of Judaism, it spoke to me about how I was feeling. If I continue trying to live my old life prior to that very sad day in July, I am not going to be successful in my new life. We must be ready to live in new ways, look at life, people, and circumstances in new ways, and ask God for help daily. New wine expands when it is fermented which stretches wine-skins. I have learned that after wine has aged, the stretched wine-skin would burst if new wine is added. I am learning to accept my new wine-skin. It is a struggle seeing myself as a new and different person. I want to love the inside as much as I love the outside. When I am able to enjoy both the inside and outside, I can celebrate.

Was anyone ever meant to witness death the way I did? Is our brain strong enough to recover from such trauma? There are no words to really describe what my eyes saw, my ears heard, my nose smelled, and my mouth said. As depression would have it, I enjoyed spending so much time with myself in complete quiet. The silence in the comfort of my bedroom is so appealing. When I am there, it seems normal. I don't hear chaos. I do not feel exposed. But wait, what is happening? What conversation am I having with myself? "Why am I here again? Where is everyone? This is not going to work because I love talking to people, and I love being with friends and family," I would say. My faith and inspirational walk has not wavered, but it is a struggle to retrain my brain on my own.

Post-Traumatic Stress Disorder, or PTSD, was once known to only include soldiers. PTSD is reaction to trauma, a reaction of anxiety. I truly believe there are hundreds of thousands of people that go undiagnosed every year. Not every person displays the same number of symptoms, but the traumatic experience really involves being part of or witnessing something horrific. I've become acquainted with certain associated behaviors and words such as isolation, triggers, flashbacks, nightmares, and memory loss.

So what does PTSD look like for me? Well, the truth is I am still finding that out. My life, in every sense of the word, has changed. No longer do things look the same through my eyes. My life has new meaning. There was a time it was easy to tell myself that I was doing fine. That my smile meant I was happy and that was the end of that. Even then, I was often hiding behind the smile and not worried that people could see through me. My self image was so important then, and I could fake it. The truth is back then, I was able to tell myself I was okay and make it believable. I was really good at it if I do say so. But as I am going through healing, I can no longer convince myself that I am fine. I look in the mirror and what looks back at me is not always outer beauty. My thoughts are not always happy. My daily regimen does not just include choosing what I will wear. Creating balance has become a challenge, but I do feel like I am winning. Because I am ready to tell myself the truth, I have given myself permission to put the pieces together one moment at a time, one emotion at time. As a truck driver in the Army Reserve, I learned the meaning of discipline and hard work. I learned that quitting is not an option. As I travel this road of rebuilding, I am finding that I am not alone. Though my trauma and tragic event is personal to me, I have discovered that so many others are striving to put their lives back in a place of peace as well. Let us work together to put our lives back together. Start telling yourself the truth about yourself and let the healing begin. I am rooting for you. I am rooting for me.

 On the morning of July 28th when my life was changed forever, I sat waiting to go meet with Stacey. She sent me a text message saying she was running late because she was still at the library and was trying to finish up some of the details. Also included in the text messages were instructions from Stacey. As usual, she was using every moment to work on the upcoming conference. She asked me to work with another committee member to gather and solidify information for the table tents we were going to have at the conference. I still have one of those emails I created a draft form on my computer. I just cannot bring myself to move it. The original plan was that I was going to meet her at her home, which was around the corner, and we would pack the car and caravan with some other friends. Since Stacey was running late, she sent a text asking if she could just come and pick me up instead. Of course, I said yes because really it made sense. We lived so close to each other, there was really not a need for me to leave my car at her home. The next memory I have was seeing Stacey back her white luxury car into my driveway and step out in a beautiful summer dress. Since it was July and we were on our way to Vegas, the multi–color halter dress was so appropriate. The colors were vibrant purples and other shades of blue. The dress was floor length, flowing in the wind, almost touching her goddess sandals. We hugged each other very tight and lovingly because we had not seen each other for a couple of months. I told her how pretty her dress was and how much I loved her new haircut. Stacey looked amazing. Her skin was glowing and her hairstyle reminded me of a "Halle Berry" look. In the five minutes it took for us to drive to her house, we talked about her Starbucks coffee (I wish I could remember the flavor) and some friends we had not seen or spoken with in a long time. We were laughing and trying to intently listen to each other. This was a great conversation between two friends. It is a conversation that one would say, under normal circumstances, was insignificant, but for me, it is one that will go on forever. In some way was Stacey protecting me by not sharing any fear she was having? If you knew you only had minutes to live, what would you do? Where would you go? Who would you want to spend time with? Even though Stacey had shared with me that her and Eddie were separated, I had planned to discuss with her options other than divorce. I had plans to ask her if she and Eddie had considered counseling. I was also prepared to talk to her about the possibility of children. There was a time when she and I discussed adoption, so I wanted to know if that would be revisited. I guess I just was not ready to see their lifelong relationship come to an end. We did a lot of things together as couples. Did I think our friendship would end? No, but I was concerned about her happiness. What I did not know or even realize is that by this time, Stacey really had made up her mind that she was not going back. She had someone that she was working with while being separated. I can now recall in one of my conversations with Stacey weeks earlier that she communicated to me, "I feel so good. I feel so free!" She said that she did not want anything from the home they shared but her shoes and her clothes. Stacey just loved shoes. Often when she was out shopping, she would call me if she saw a pair I might like. The joke was always on me because I have such tiny feet. Stacey called once because she was so excited about the pair she found for me that she had to text me a picture! I really did like the shoes, and she wanted me to meet her in Santa Ana to pick them up. I still have the shoes and wear them periodically. She was just always thinking of others.

Along with other couples, we would spend birthdays together; we shared holidays together. We loved to laugh. When Stacey's family would visit from out of state, we would plan get-togethers that included food and games. Stacey loved playing board games and having friendly competitions. One thing I especially loved about Stacey was her willingness to help inspire others. She was never afraid to share information that could help someone else achieve their goals. That is how her non-profit organization, Pink Ladder, was started. She always had a charitable spirit and honorable intentions. Nothing Stacey did, to my knowledge, was self-serving. Motives must be pure and not about the recognition. I would challenge you as well as myself—the next time an opportunity to give represents itself, ask yourself this question, "Would I still do this if no would ever know I did it?" Examine your value system. It is important for us to know what we actually value and if we are spending our time and energy on goals that reflect our values. So let's complete an exercise together. First, create a list of 10 things you value the most. Is it family? Is it your appearance? What about your health? Job? Your independence? Now that you have your list of 10 written down, next I want you to do an evaluation to find out which are the most important values to you from that list. I want you to do a side-by-side comparison for each value. In comparing them with each other, if you could only have 5 of the 10 values you have listed, which 5 would you choose? For example, if you had to choose between your job and your family, which would you choose? If you had to choose between your independence and personal growth, which would you choose? Rebuilding life may change our value system as we are progressing. By understanding your values, you will be able to more easily set goals for your future. I would even encourage you to create a mission statement. Once you create your mission statement, put

Keep Good Records of Repairs

it in a place where you can read it often. Your personal mission statement will remind you of the person you are becoming.

Sitting in the car is something most of us do every day without thinking of it as being of any significance. I often will sit a few extra minutes when I pull into my garage. I don't know about you, but I need that time to breathe in, breathe out, and begin again. Every so often, my youngest will say, "Mom, when we get home, can you get out of the car quickly because I am really hungry!" Of course, I tell him that I will be in shortly after I take my minute.

There was nothing that seemed odd or different when we made it to Stacey and Eddie's home and backed into the garage right next to Eddie's car. I recall that Stacey did not seem the least bit surprised. I remember that when she pulled in my driveway to pick me up, she was speaking to someone on the phone and I heard her say she was picking me up. Was she talking to Eddie? Was he asking her if we were on our way? As soon as we exited the car, Stacey closed the garage door. This did not seem strange to me at all because some homeowner's associations may require the homeowner to keep the garage doors closed. It was hot, however, and I was not sure how I was going to ask Stacey for some ventilation. Deep down, I think she knew how warm it was because she propped open the single door that separated us from the inside of the home. So why was Eddie home? I thought maybe he was home to see Stacey because she had been away for a couple of months. We all spoke as one would normally, by offering warm greetings. I think Eddie and I even hugged before we began packing Stacey's car just as we had intended. Several boxes were inside the house and Stacey would go on to ask Eddie if he would not mind bringing them out to the car. He agreed and even offered to load the car with the various conference materials. I do recall him asking if she wanted to go inside to get anything from inside. She nonchalantly and calmly answered by saying no. Eddie continued to have a casual conversation about the mail. There did not seem to be anything unusual or strange about the communication. At one point, he tried handing Stacey the mail, but she was quite busy on the phone speaking with one of the Pink Ladder committee members. The group wanted to be sure we were still on schedule to depart to Vegas. Now, some people may have believed that Eddie and Stacey argued while being in the garage. I can confirm that there was no arguing or a loud tone whatsoever. As Stacey and I printed conference materials, the mood in the garage was very calm. Among other things, she was planning our lunch and giving one of our friend's directions to her home because we were all preparing to caravan. While holding that conversation, Stacey was also saving all of the last minute updates for the conference on her laptop with one hand and was having me do a repeat printing of the name placards of the conference attendees. To her, some of the names looked crooked and not aligned.

Stacey loved Pink Ladder. As the founder and visionary, she was determined to make each year better than the last. It was not because she wanted it to be bigger, but she wanted to offer more inspiration to other women who were trying to achieve and climb the ladder of success. After one of the first Pink Ladder Step-Up Conferences, Stacey shared a book with all of the women who attended that year. I just found that book and the letter. In the letter, she thanked all of us for making the conference such a success. Stacey asked us to continue to follow our goals and keep encouraging each other.

When I had finally gotten the hang of making the placards perfect on the copier, I felt relaxed and maybe even distracted. I was trying to become invisible only because I did not want to seem like I was paying attention to any conversations Eddie and Stacey might be having. There was a moment when Eddie had to help with the printer because it was not printing correctly due to the way it was installed. Stacey had recently purchased a new laptop, and it needed to have the copier added. Nothing seemed out of the ordinary, and we were just about complete with the printing and loading the conference materials in the back of Stacey's car. This whole process did not take long at all. The sound of the copier was like soft music until the calm was disturbed by the loudest ringing sound I ever heard. Time just stopped and stood still for a few seconds. Out of the corner of my right eye I saw that my friend Stacey had fallen. She was not moving, and I couldn't see her face because she was behind Eddie's motorcycle. Then, above my head, I saw smoke. Wait! Did the copier break down? Oh no, I could now smell something that I had not smelled in a long time. Gun smoke!

Still not quite sure of what just happened, I turned to my left and there I saw what I just could not believe. Eddie was holding the shiniest gun I had ever seen. My first words were, "Oh my God, oh my God!" Pointing the gun, Eddie told me not to move because he was not going to hurt me. Eddie then proceeded to look around me to Stacey. What was he thinking? Was he checking for movement? Would he dare to shoot Stacey again? In those few seconds, I looked into Eddie's eyes. He was no longer my friend. I did not recognize that person. Those eyes were cold, and his face had no expression. Is it possible to see inside of a person's soul? What was he contemplating in that moment? The next words that would come from his mouth were, "I am going to go inside and shoot myself, and when I do, you can leave. And I am sorry." I was able to say, "Okay, Eddie I am not going to move, I am not going to go anywhere, I promise", hysterically. I am imagining I was panic-stricken and paralyzed at the same time. Even as I thought to myself that I could get out of that garage, my feet would not move. The three-car garage doors were closed, and I was inside with Stacey on the ground near the front of the third garage door. There was also a motorcycle and two cars. Anything could have happened next. I chose to believe Eddie in those few moments, and I did not move. Then Eddie did just what he said. I watched him slowly back away from me, enter the house, and lock the door behind him. My heart was racing, and my hands were sweating. Since Eddie was no longer in the garage, what was I waiting on? I knew that my purse and my cell phone were in Stacey's car. I was not close enough to grab them. I was thinking about Stacey behind me, and I didn't think she had moved. Should I have started running? Should I have gone behind the motorcycle to see about Stacey? In the next few moments, my nerves got the best of me because I thought I heard Eddie coming back for me in the garage so I quickly yell out, "I have not moved Eddie, I am still here!" Then it happened…another gunshot…

The second gunshot was just as shocking as the first. "Oh my God! Oh my God! Eddie just shot himself!" I had to get to Stacey's car to get to my cell phone which was on the front seat. Hurriedly, I opened the passenger car door and scrambled to grab my purse. I had to get out of the garage to get help! Did anyone hear the gun shots? How long had it been since he shot Stacey? I had my purse, and I pulled out my phone before I exited the garage. Next, I opened the side door from the garage but really struggled to get the side gate opened. "Help, please, somebody help!" In the next few minutes of frantically calling 911, my husband, and the other friends that were close to Stacey, I remember thinking this could not be happening. Why now, God? Why was I there? Why did this happen? Is this real? Why didn't he kill me? Why did he tell me he was sorry? How could this be? All questions that I may never have the answers to in this life. The next phase of my new reality was just a daze. I think to myself that maybe, just maybe, I was present for Stacey so that I could report to her family that she died suddenly and there was no more violence. And maybe I was not there for her at all. Maybe I was there for Eddie. I really do not remember some of the things I said or did in the days and weeks that followed because maybe I was silent for the most part. I just know that I cried and cried and cried. My children knew something was different. My husband and I met with our teenage son because we thought he could process it. My stubbornness would not let me cry in front of my children, but they did witness some of my anxious behavior. I was so sad, and I felt helpless and could not pull myself out of it. Sure, I had lots of visits, phone calls, cards, and people praying, but I just could not break from my sadness and my tears. Nobody knew what I was going through. I felt so alone. I would just keep saying. I just did not like what I saw in the mirror. I tried to figure out why my life had been spared. What was it about me, because I just could not see it.

Chapter 5

Focus on One Rebuild at a Time

I still have visions of what that moment in the garage looked like, and with the help of a prayer warrior in Detroit, Michigan, that vision was brought into view. This special prayer warrior that I was meeting with for first time told me she saw angels watching over me in that moment. I literally saw these angels swirling as she was praying over me the weekend of Stacey's funeral. But I also saw one strong angel and had a vision of this angel with his hands on my shoulders, keeping me still because Eddie asked me not to move. It really looked like a picture found in a comic book. "I knew it!" I said, "I knew I was not alone in that moment!" Psalms 23 verses 1 through 4 have taken on more of a meaning to me. *"Jehovah is my shepherd; I shall not want. He maketh me to lie down in green pastures; He leadeth me beside still waters. He restoreth my soul; He guideth me in the paths of righteousness for his name's sake. Yea, though I walk through the valley of the shadow of death, I will fear no evil; for thou art with me; Thy rod and thy staff, they comfort me."*

In this Psalm, the author David shares that God is a caring shepherd. When death is upon us, it may feel and look like a dark presence and dark shadow. When trauma or heart ache or life's challenges or the end of a relationship are staring at us, we can only trust in our training whatever that may be. I am sometimes reminded of my fears, my heartaches, my pain, and my shortcomings, but because God is walking beside me and leading me, I know that my steps are being ordered. Life is uncertain, but I am trusting in my shepherd. Find your inner peace whether it is through praying, fasting, or meditating. Work to find a sweet place rebuilding one trauma at a time.

So when it got to be the middle of August and I was still very sad, I just knew there was something else going on with me. I was not able to leave the house without feeling like everyone was looking at me and waiting to see what I was going to say or do. I was still spending the entire day at home in my room on my bed, and at some point, I would remember that I had not eaten anything. Sure, I was praying, but I still felt so alone. Why was I not able to snap out of it? Why couldn't I get back to being a wife and mother? I really did want to go to choir rehearsal and fulfill my other obligations. But I was so tired, and I just wanted to rest. I lay in bed, and then it was morning. I did not get any sleep.

I tried so hard, but the vision of that day kept playing in my head over and over and over. I knew at this point that I had to see a doctor. But wait, if I saw a doctor, did that mean something was wrong with me? I did not know how I felt about that. But I did need to talk to someone. I tried talking to my husband. Bless his heart, I know he was trying to help me, but it was not working. He was listening, but this was new to him as well. The victims program I was registered with offered all of us great resources on how to process the grief. The recommendations were specific to how my husband and children should respond and support me.

Something I have not shared to this point is that I am pretty shy and private when it comes to my emotions. I do not like anyone seeing me cry. I really want to stay away from everyone until I can get myself together. It is very uncomfortable being around people and trying to hold my emotions inside and at the same time have people asking me if I am okay or if I'm alright now. How do you answer? These are just a few of the questions I am still trying to work through with my counselor. One thing I am sure of is I will not be successful in rebuilding without the right support. I have my church family, my prayer life, my husband, my friends, and even the busyness of my job, but without the counseling, my rebuilding while in recovery would be even harder. I am in search of healthy relationships and not just someone that is trying to be helpful. What I mean by that has to do with people that I feel are pressuring me to hurry and move on. Maybe from the outside it appears that I am faking or trying to look depressed and sad? Who determines when my sadness is over? Are people really that insensitive? I know I am trying to do what I can to accept the fact that I am not the same person. This experience has forced me to look at my life and even pick it apart. I am starting from scratch.

The first few sessions with my therapist were just about me crying and retelling the story over and over. I just wanted to know how to get the visions from replaying over and over in my head. The visions would always start with the gunshot, Stacey falling, and me turning to see the gun in Eddie's hand. Then the vision would start all over again. This vision consumed my every minute of the day. I found myself trying to shake it off. What could the therapist share with me to help me sleep and move forward? The office was cold and stark. From the start of therapy, I did not enjoy the experience. By the second session, I quickly noticed that the therapist was distant and never even wanted to shake my hand. After four sessions, I just could not do it anymore. Even if I was going to have to pay,

I needed to find a therapist that could relate to me. In the beginning, I thought I was hurting her feelings if I would stop our visits, but then my victim's advocate helped me realize that I needed to feel comfortable. So, I asked for my advocate's help in finding that right fit. I was lucky that the next one I contacted was the right fit. We bonded and connected from the very start. She was warm and seemed to care about my healing. My new therapist seemed to understand me when I showed emotion, and that is what I needed. She was also able to tell me the truth in what I was sharing. I needed help to move past the tragic events of July 28th. I was now also beginning to realize that my life as a mother and as a wife was being challenged, and some issues would need to be addressed outside of this therapy session as well. Who wants to hear that they have issues? If you want to rebuild your life after a traumatic experience, you do! I do! As a wife and mother, I just have to keep going. I want to get better for them. I want to be better for me. They need me, and that is why rebuilding is the only option. One thing I realized in late September of that year was I had begun to hold back my emotions. I became so busy with life my mood changed towards so many things. I was yelling more at home. I was losing my temper but at the same time paranoid that no one cared about what I was going through. I just felt like being alone. I know this was not right, but it is what I wanted.

My therapist asked if I was ready for the next step in my treatment. Of course, because things were going well with my therapy I told her I was ready. She introduced me to Eye Movement Desensitization and Reprocessing or EMDR treatment. The goal of this treatment is to help a person process and recall a traumatic event that is causing difficulty. The idea is that I would try to replace those visions that were causing me so much stress with positive images and thoughts. I would attempt to put those negative emotions on a shelf. I have read that EMDR was created initially to assist those experiencing Post-Traumatic Stress Disorder or PTSD.

I began the treatment, and I will just say that my head was spinning in circles. I did not know what to expect. It was intense. I did feel the emotion. I asked my therapist to slow down the intensity if she could. Part of the EMDR treatment was having to go back to the event itself in my mind as I listened to these soft sounds in my ear. I found that to be pretty difficult. I had questions all over again. I wanted to know why it happened. Having to learn how to put these thoughts away and not letting it take over my mind was going to take more time. I knew the Lord was equipping me because I am a work in progress. EMDR proved to be too much for me at that time, but I do believe in the treatment. My therapist did ask me to try it one more time before I completely gave up. She was trying to help me get rid of the replay of the tragic event of witnessing the loss of Stacey and Eddie. I did try it one more time. This time, I practiced slowing my breathing. It was not easy, and it was not fun. My heart was racing and my hands were sweaty. I found myself so sad after that session and that told me that I was not ready, so I opted to end my EMDR sessions. In the time since the EMDR process, I began to have other more positive visions. I am now able to replace the tragic effects in my memory-replay. My visions allow me to see images of Stacey, the time we spent together in the car, and how good she looked. I am retraining my brain to not think of the negative and see trouble when the flashes come. I do not have to see the bad because I can choose to remember how happy Stacey was in her final moments.

Rebuilding life means facing my fears.

Chapter 6

Expect Aftershocks

The annual Word Women's Conference hosted by my church was coming up, and I knew I wanted to go. I had to fight the urge to stay home. I decided to go, and I am so glad I did. My decision to only have one roommate was also the right decision. She and I prayed together. Her angelic spirit was gentle, and I felt no pressure. What I really needed more than anything was rest and a chance to be ministered to. I discovered that rebuilding life means facing your fears. During that conference, I was able to let go and lower the wall I unintentionally built. I cried out! I released my fears and decided that I was going to deal with the aftershocks as they came. When you expect the aftershocks that will come, often those events, in comparison to an earthquake, are less violent or traumatic. But they may still trigger a setback. These aftershocks can occur in the first hours, days, weeks, months, years.

From the moment I made it to the conference, I felt the spirit of calmness. It was on the last day that I was really able to cry out in public and not care who saw or heard me. I do truly believe this really is where my true healing began. The next stage of my rebuilding came in January at Convocation where Rev. Battle, a visiting minister from New Jersey, preached a sermon, "Called to Faithfulness", from John 10 beginning at the 16th verse. God was speaking to me through that message in such a way I do not think He ever had before. He told me that there was a calling on my life. He told me that the ending of the old life is the beginning of the new life and that Christian faith is all about the beginning. We are in "Worker Readiness Training." The scripture that really spoke to me from this passage was verse 28. ***Jesus said, "and I give unto them eternal life; and they shall never perish and no one shall snatch them out of my hand."*** What this verse is saying to me is do not be afraid of those who want to kill your body; they cannot touch your soul. Fear only God who can destroy both soul and body. And if you believe in life after death as I do, I know that Stacey is with the Lord in heaven. Whether you are someone who lives by Christian principles or someone that just has meditation methods, know that your life is not your own. You have been blessed to bless others. Build a legacy that will come after you.

Expect Aftershocks

So why did Eddie tell me he was sorry after he shot my friend? I ask myself that question a lot. I just do not have an answer. I know that to this point, I have not said much about Eddie, but he was my friend as well. I enjoyed spending time around him and showing him God's love through how I interacted with him. We did not always agree on business practices, but I do think he listened to me. Once, he asked me about church and why we drove so far. Then weeks later, Eddie joined us on a Sunday. He told my husband later he and Stacey enjoyed the service, but it was just too far to drive. Now, I do not want to say that Eddie was a religious man, but I do know that he did feel a longing to know Christ.

When I turned 40, I wanted to have a birthday celebration. I wanted to have a room full of close family and friends with lots of food and fun. Stacey could not help me plan because at the time she was traveling a lot but did say she and Eddie would be the first ones there. They were! The first ones there before we were even done with all of the decorations. She had just gotten off a plane and had Eddie to meet her at the party. Both Eddie and Stacey looked so happy that warm Friday night in March. I have so many pictures from that evening at the Hilton Hotel. I was so happy that I felt the need to have the party. The party brought together so many of the people we had not seen for such a long time. My closest friends and co-workers, my family that flew in from Illinois, my church family, members from the gospel recording group I toured with, and my sorority sisters all took time to be with me for some great food, games, and dancing. Because our jobs and family lives became so hectic, we just did not get together as often.

In April, while Stacey, a few of our friends, and I celebrated Eddie's birthday at their Birdhollow residence, Eddie and I had some time to talk. We laughed about some of the things that happened at my party, and we shared about how I planned and prepared for the celebration. I commented on how I had a vision of 100 people being in attendance. I told him that I sent out enough invites to have that many guests and even over planned the number because I was sure some people would not be able to show. Well, when just about everyone responded with a confirmation of attendance, I told Eddie that I began to panic because we could not go over 100. I will never forget what Eddie said to me next. He said, "Tonya, you are a good person. Of course people want to come celebrate with you. If I were having a party, I do not think anyone would come." Was Eddie sending me a message? My response to him, "Oh, Eddie, you should not say that. Of course people would come to help you celebrate." That was the end of the conversation. As I drove home that evening, I reflected on that conversation. When I mentioned it to my husband, we thought Eddie was being really sincere. I prayed that night that Eddie would not feel that people would not want to celebrate with him. I prayed that God would fill his heart with love and that he would be able to address any issues he may have had with any of his friends. That was in the month of April; Eddie killed himself in July. Was there anything else I could have said or done in April?

While officers conducted their investigation after the murder-suicide, several items were found that were used to piece together some of the major events. In a typed letter that was found in the home of Eddie and Stacey, Eddie quoted that he and Stacey's love was one that was forever. He wrote to his closest family and friends. I guess somehow he believed that we would someday read it. Eddie says in the letter that no one was at fault and for us not to be sad for him. He had believed he let everyone down and that he was somehow flawed. He went on to say to Stacey that he loved her and that he was remorseful and regretful for some of the things he had done. Eddie also said to his friends and made reference to some family members that he was sorry that he did not do more to mend and fix relationships. Lastly, Eddie's final words from the letter that are forever etched in my memory were, "Live life and prosper as I know you will."

In the last moments of Eddie asking me not to move, I wonder if I would have tried to reason with him, could the outcome have been different. Everything happened so fast that I do not feel I could have asked him anything. What I am telling you is that chaos can occur when things are calm. My life has changed forever. Some may say that justice was served because Eddie died as well. But I believe a person dying does not automatically bring you closure or give justice to your situation or circumstance. Eddie said to me, "Do not move; I am not going to hurt you." This makes sense because there was a gun and you have been told you are not going to get hurt. When I examine my life since that moment, I find that I hurt the most when I am not moving. Now, what do I mean by that? When I am working, when I am with my husband or with the boys, or even when I am in therapy or support group, I am moving. When I am not moving, I am at home, it is late at night, and my mind starts to race. I start to cry. I become anxious and alone with my thoughts. No one else is in that space but me. This can be very emotional, depressing, and sad. This is what I continue to work through. Seeking assistance is part of the process and helps you cope. This is usually a gradual process for our mental and physical being. Assistance is available, and knowing how to access it makes the process move faster and can be less stressful.

Recently, my youngest son asked me if he could wear my eye glasses. He said they look really cool on me, and he wanted to see how they would look on him. Of course when he put them on he said, "Hey! One eye is blurry; I cannot see!" This reminded me that we love the idea of "one size fits all" and often forget that we view life through our own set of lenses based on our own eye examination. The prescription is unique to our vision. My son then proceeded to ask, "Well, Mom do you have any other pairs? Can I try on a different color?" I guess he was thinking that if he changed the color of the frame, the style of the glasses, the vision would not be blurred. Now, he is under 10 years of age and has not realized that no matter how many times he put on my frames, my vision would never match his vision. I shared that story because I continue to think about the rebuilding process. There is not going to be a "one size fits all" technique. My trauma is different than your trauma. My sadness is different than your sadness. My healing will be different from your healing. Progress is possible. It may be painful, but it is possible.

Not long after Stacey died, I was introduced by my close spiritual friend and victim's advocate to an awesome group of people. I connected with a support group that is such a blessing. It is called Parents of Murdered Children or POMC. This is a national organization, and the support group welcomes anyone who has lost a relative, friend, or loved one to violence. There are so many support groups, but I also know it is important to find one where you feel connected. In this group, I am able to cry without the feelings of judgment. I am able to experience the various emotions I go through, and there are others who share the same emotions as I. Annually, POMC welcomes friends and loved ones to a candlelight vigil and names dedication ceremony. Family members and friends are invited to have the name of their loved one etched on a placard and remembered in a memorial garden. Stacey's name was dedicated, and her nephew, along with some of her other close friends and my family, were in attendance honoring her memory. This was a big step in my rebuilding. Admittedly, there is not anything that I am experiencing in my rebuilding that is easy. I have stopped saying that I just wanted to go back to the old me because I know that is impossible. If you really stop and think, I died that day with Stacey and Eddie. It is hard letting go of the old me, but I am up for the challenge.

Rebuilding life requires acceptance of the new you

I am becoming more patient with the new me every day. Some days are good and some days are a struggle, but I am encouraged each day because I have been given a new day. Rebuilding life requires acceptance of the new you. Each day is unique and carries its own recovery. My life is a testimony that I am willing to share if it means helping anyone get into recovery to rebuild their life because of the hurts in this world. My daily walk is even more personal because my pain and progress is personal.

So what is my encouragement to you? Find the right support. You want to surround yourself with people who mean you well. You want people who will be a healthy support as opposed to just trying to be helpful. Find quiet time to stay away. I pray and offer up petitions of thanksgiving. It is important to know that our lives, your life, my life, are not just lived for us. A scripture that is close to my heart, **"And let us not be weary in well-doing; for in due season we shall reap, if we faint not", Galatians 6:9.** This is not just speaking of receiving a monetary reward, but your harvest can be the healing of your broken heart. Your harvest can be finding peace after the death of a loved-one or even having the ability to forgive someone like your spouse who you feel has hurt you deeply.

Rebuilding my life is about doing something I have never done. A lot of the pieces to rebuilding are already there. It is about reconstruction from the inside out. See your healing and believe in your floor plan, but more importantly, you have to accept that you will have a future of firsts. Decide to retrain the brain to create new memories. When change is for the better, focus on faith and not fears. Make adjustments as needed and create the best you with your resources. Believe boldly and pray passionately. See it, say it, script it! I am not where I want to be, but I am getting there! The best is yet to come!

Resources

The month of October has been named as the National Domestic Violence Awareness Month. The best way to end the violence is by getting involved, becoming more educated, and by supporting your local and national efforts.

> National Crime Victims' Rights Week (April)
> Office of Justice Programs/Office for Victims of Crime
> http://ovc.ncjrs.gov/ncvrw/
>
> National Domestic Violence Hotline
> (800) 799-7233
> http://www.thehotline.org/
>
> National Organization of Parents of Murdered Children
> (888) 818-7662
> http://www.pomc.com/

National Suicide Prevention Lifeline
(800) 273-talk (8255)
http://www.suicidepreventionlifeline.org/

About the Author

Tonya L. Whiteside has love and passion to work with people. She is an educator for high school students in the area of career and technical education teaching Small Business Management and Entrepreneurship, and for over 12 years, a high school academic advisor. Tonya also has more than 20 years of experience in presenting workshops and inspiring young people. A former Facilitator and Workshop Presenter for Monster.com's Diversity Leadership Program (DLP), Tonya speaks and trains on topics such as: job readiness, career development, workplace diversity, customer service, team building, and leadership.

The Hopkins Park, IL native is an Army Reserve Veteran and continues to volunteer working with her local "Future Soldier" program. Other community service involvement includes being an active member of the Friendship Baptist Church located in Yorba Linda, CA, Delta Sigma Theta Sorority, Inc. Orange County Alumnae Chapter, and a trained Domestic Violence Advocate and volunteer for Laura's House, a domestic violence agency in South Orange County that provides residential shelter services, life skills education, counseling, and legal services to hundreds of women and children.

Tonya is the founder of The Whiteside Group and the award winning author of *Change the Atmosphere with Encouraging Words*. She really loves being a wife and mother. Tonya resides in Southern California with her husband Earnest and two sons.

ALSO AVAILABLE:

Can be found:
http://www.amazon.com
Barnes and Noble Stores
http://www.barnesandnoble.com/
http://www.thewhitesidegroup.net
wherever eBooks are sold

Contact Information

Tonya L. Whiteside is available for speaking engagements, support groups, book club discussions, and workshops. For availability and additional information, contact:

Tonya L. Whiteside
The Whiteside Group
31441 Santa Margarita Pkwy., Ste., A #344
Rancho Santa Margarita, CA 92688

Website: http://www.thewhitesidegroup.net
Email: tonya@thewhitesidegroup.net

www.ingramcontent.com/pod-product-compliance
Ingram Content Group UK Ltd.
Pitfield, Milton Keynes, MK11 3LW, UK
UKHW041955230426
12048UKWH00008B/343